ABIDE WITH ME;
FAST FALLS THE EVENTIDE
A Sung Prayer of the Christian Tradition

ABIDE WITH ME;
FAST FALLS THE EVENTIDE
A Sung Prayer of the Christian Tradition

Samuel J. Rogal

The History of Christian Hymnody
Volume 9

The Edwin Mellen Press
Lewiston•Queenston•Lampeter

Library of Congress Cataloging-in-Publication Data

Abide with me; fast falls the eventide : a sung prayer of the Christian tradition / Samuel J. Rogal.
    p. cm. -- (The history of Christian hymnody ; v. 9)
  Includes bibliographical references.

ISBN 0-7734-0844-4

1. Protestant churches--Hymns--History and criticism. 2. Hymns--History and criticism. 3. Lyte, Henry Francis, 1793-1847. 4.Monk, William Henry, 1823-1889. Abide with me. I. Title.
ML3100.R63 2009
264'.23092--dc22

2009032421

This is volume 9 in the continuing series
History of Christian Hymnody

HCH Series ISBN-13: 978-0-7734-3903-0
HCH Series ISBN-10: 0-7734-3903-X

A CIP catalog record for this book is available from the British Library.

Copyright © 2010 Samuel J. Rogal

All rights reserved. For information contact

      The Edwin Mellen Press   The Edwin Mellen Press
             Box 450   Box 67
      Lewiston, New York   Queenston, Ontario
       USA 14092-0450   CANADA L0S 1L0

The Edwin Mellen Press, Ltd.
Lampeter, Ceredigion, Wales
UNITED KINGDOM SA48 8LT

Printed in the United States of America

Abide with me; fast falls the eventide.
The darkness thickens; Lord, with me abide!
When other helpers fail, and comforts flee,
Help of the helpless, O abide with me.

Table of Contents

Abide With Me; Fast Falls the Eventide (1847)

1. The Text	1
2. Introduction to the Hymn	2
3. The Text as Poem	7
4. The Text as Congregational Hymn	11
5. The Text in Hymn Book and Hymnal	18
6. Henry Francis Lyte (1793-1847): His Life	23
7. Henry Francis Lyte: Hymnodist	26
8. The Hymn Tunes and Their Composers	29
9. Personal Reaction	37
10. List of Works Cited and Consulted	39

Abide With Me;
Fast Falls the Eventide

1. The Text

Abide with Me; Fast Falls the Eventide (1847)

1. Abide with me; fast falls the eventide,
   The darkness thickens; Lord, with me abide!
   When other helpers fail, and comforts flee,
   Help of the helpless, O abide with me.

2. Swift to its close ebbs out life's little day;
   Earth's joys grow dim, its glories pass away;
   Change and decay in all around I see;
   O Thou who changest not, abide with me.

3. Not a brief glance I beg, a passing word;
   But as Thou dwell'st with Thy disciples, Lord,
   Familiar, condescending, patient, free,
   Come not to sojourn, but abide with me!

4. Come not in terrors as the King of Kings,
   But kind and good, with healing in Thy wings,
   Tears for all woes, a heart for every plea,--
   Come, Friend of sinners, and thus bide with me.

5. Thou on my head in early youth did smile:
   And, though rebellious and perverse meanwhile,
   Thou hast not left me, oft as I left Thee.
   On to the close, O Lord, abide with me!

1. Abide with me; fast falls the eventide,
   The darkness thickens; Lord, with me abide!
   When other helpers fail, and comforts flee,

Help of the helpless, O abide with me.

2 Swift to its close ebbs out life's little day;
Earth's joys grow dim, its glories pass away;
Change and decay in all around I see;
O Thou who changest not, abide with me.

6 I need Thy presence every passing hour;
What but Thy grace can foil the tempter's power?
Who like Thyself my guide and stay can be?
Through cloud and sunshine, Lord, O abide with me!

7 I fear no foe with Thee at hand to bless;
Ills have no weight, and tears no bitterness;
Where is death's sting? where, grave, Thy victory?
I triumph still, if Thou abide with me.

8 Hold, then, Thy Cross before my closing eyes;
Speak through the gloom and point me to the skies;
Heav'n's morning breaks, and earth's vain shadows flee;
In life, in death, O Lord, abide with me.[1]

2. Introduction to the Hymn

Information concerning the composition of congregational hymns--both texts and tunes--can easily flow off into different directions and emphases, depending upon the degrees by which hymnologists and biographers wish to

---

[1] Source: *Hymns Ancient and Modern, for Use in the Services of the Church. With Accompanying Tunes.* Historical Edition (London: William Clowes and Sons, Limited, 1909): 30 (hymn 23). The editors' version of the text, derived from the author's manuscript, then in possession of his grandson, Cecil Maxwell Lyte, consists of stanzas 1, 2, 6, 7, 8 of the complete hymn; however, they do cite stanzas 3, 4, and 5 in their accompanying note., citing changes and thus providing a complete text of the piece. One will also see the full text, in proper and full order, in Edmund Clarence Stedman (ed.), *A Victorian Anthology (1837-1895). Selections Illustrating the Editor's Critical Review of British Poetry in the Reign of Victoria* (Boston and New York: Houghton, Mifflin and Company, 1896): 173-174.

manipulate their readers' emotions or to convince them of facts. For, as every churchgoer knows, hymn singing can (and should, for that matter) become a highly emotional exercise. The details that surround the composition of Henry Francis Lyte's "Abide with me; fast falls the eventide" form a fairly consistent theses, but, unfortunately, not all of those details that have been offered for public scrutiny appear to find concrete support. Thus, if at all possible, the reasonable needs to be siphoned from the emotional to determine why and how Henry Francis Lyte composed this classic piece.

In 1889, the Rev. R.E. Welsh, of St. George's, Brondesbury, London, and his co-author, F.G. Edwards, claimed that Lyte had been asked to attend the death-bed of a neighboring Devonshire (?) clergyman who realized the approach of his end, but had not been sufficiently prepared for the transition from mortality to wherever one goes following his or her last breath. According to Welsh and Edwards, Lyte, also, found himself unprepared for the experience, and so together they explored the Pauline epistles "in search of peace and hope." Lyte later reported that his colleague "died happy under the belief that, though he had deeply erred, there was One Whose death and sufferings would atone for his delinquencies, and he accepted for all that he incurred." The hymnodist also confessed that the cleric's passing deeply affected him, causing him to study his Bible and to preach "in another manner than I had previously done." He even assumed charge of the departed's children and increased his activity as a writer of hymns--all of that under the physical stress of ill health, which eventually necessitated his removal to the southern and warmer climate of Nice, France.

On the morning prior to his departure (again, according to Welsh and Edwards), Lyte stood before his congregation at Lower Brixham, on the southern coast of Devonshire, to celebrate the Holy Supper and to deliver a parting address: "I stand before you seasonably to-day, as alive from the dead, as I may hope to impress it upon you, and indulge you to prepare for that solemn hour which must come to all, by a timely acquaintance with, appreciation of, and dependence on, the death of Christ." Afterward, he departed to his quarters, remaining there long enough to write the eight stanzas that began, "Abide with me; fast falls the eventide,/The darkness thickens; Lord, with me abide!" [2]

A second pair of hymnologists, the Americans Theron Brown and Hezekiah Butterworth, who produced a similar book some seventeen years later, indicated only that Lyte spent a lifetime suffering from consumption, and that on the evening of his final Sunday of preaching he "handed to one of his family the manuscript of his hymn, 'Abide with me,' and the music he had composed for it."[3] A year later, in 1907, Dr. John Julian, vicar of Topcliffe, in the North Riding of Yorkshire, at that time the leading scholar among the hymnologists, gathered his details as to the composition of "Abide with me" from Lyte's daughter, Anna Maria Maxwell Hogg, who had written the "Memoir" to her father's *Remains* (London: Rivington, 1850). According to that essay, Lyte delivered that last sermon on the Holy Communion on Sunday, 4 September 1847, in extremely weakened condition, but yet managed to administer the Holy Eucharist. Although "necessarily much exhausted by the exertion and excitement, yet his friends had no reason to believe it had been hurtful to him. In the evening of the same day he placed in the hands of a near and dear relative the little hymn, 'Abide with me,' with an air of his own composing, adapted to the words." Perhaps Mrs. Hogg needed to be told that thirty-two lines comprised considerably more than merely "a little hymn." At any rate, although Dr. Julian did recount the anecdote of the dying neighboring clergyman whom Lyte had comforted, but he connected it only to Lyte's spiritual change rather than to extending its meaning further and onto

---

[2] R.E. Welsh and F.G. Edwards, *The Romance of Psalter and Hymnal: Authors and Composers* (London: Hodder and Stoughton, 1889): 163-168. The authors never cite the sources for the passages that they quote.
[3] Theron Brown and Hezekiah Butterworth, *The Story of the Hymns and Tunes* (New York: American Tract Society, 1906): 217.

his classic hymn, as had Welsh and Edwards.[4]

The compilers of the 1909 "Historical Edition" of *Hymns Ancient and Modern* supplied a slightly different perspective to what they labelled the "touching circumstances" relative to the composition of Lyte's hymn. The following passage, although without quotation marks or credit to a source, obviously had been appropriated, in part, from the same account by Mrs. Hogg cited in Dr. Julian's entry: "At the age of fifty-four, he [Lyte] was dying of consumption, and in sorrow at having to leave his work unfinished, he prayed that he might be able to write something which should live to the glory of God, when he was dead. On the last Sunday in September [1847] he ministered to his flock at Brixham for the last time, and in the evening of the same day he placed in the hands of a near and dear relative the Hymn 'Abide with me,' with an air of his own composing adapted to the words."[5] One can only speculate as to what caused the compilers of the 1909 *Hymns Ancient and Modern* to change the date of composition from 4 September 1747 to the "last Sunday in September."

Two decades following the publication of the "Historical Edition" of *Hymns Ancient and Modern*, Professor John Dahle of the Luther Theological Seminary, St. Paul, Minnesota, the leading hymnologist in the Norwegian Lutheran Church of America, produced a three-volume guide to the most common hymns embraced by Protestants. In terms of "Abide with me," Dahle determined that "The history of this hymn ought to begin with the words of Lyte's daughter, Anna Maria Maxwell Hogg, written by her in the preface to *Lyte's Remains*, published after his death (London, 1850)."[6] Professor Dahle did not actually extend the background discussion beyond the lengthy quotation from Mrs. Hogg's

---

[4] John Julian, *A Dictionary of Hymnology*, 2nd rev. ed., with Supplement (London: John Murray, 1907; rpt. New York: Dover Publications, Inc., 1957), 1:7, 706.
[5] *Hymns Ancient and Modern* (1909), 30.
[6] John Dahle, *Library of Christian Hymns*, trans. M. Casper Johnshoy (Minneapolis, Minnesota: Augsburg Publishing House, 1928), 3:750-751.

"Preface"--a replication of the language that one finds in Dr. Julian's account, and thus the former's "beginning" yields no fresh ending.

Finally, by 1979, the Reverend Professor John Monteith Barkley, Ph.D., Professor of Church history and Symbolics at the Presbyterian College, Belfast, Ireland, with "much assistance from diocesan registrars, the secretaries of societies, and individual scholars on a wide variety of details," introduced what appeared to be a totally new beam of light onto the background details relative to Lyte's hymn. Barkley, initially, nodded in the direction of the "tradition" for Lyte having written the piece on 4 September 1847, "just before he left his parish at Brixham, Devon, to go to Nice, dying there on 20 November following." Then, abruptly, he cited an article in a 1925 issue of *The Spectator* to the effect that Lyte had written "Abide with me" in *1820*, after a visit to a dying friend, one William Le Hunte, who kept repeating the phrase "Abide with me."[7] Not content with that claim, Barkley turned to yet another source, a letter written by Lyte to Eleanor Julia Bolton (who would marry his son in 1851), dated 25 August 1847. Lyte, in that epistle, mentioned "Abide with me" as "my latest effusion."[8] However, since Barkley failed to indicate the locale of that letter, and since he quoted only three words from it, his beacon of new light on the matter dims quickly. One might wish to end the issue by acknowledging that, in its compilation of "Hymnodic Anniversaries," the Hymn Society of the United States and Canada continues to place "Abide with me" within the year 1847--the year of its composition.[9] Insofar as *publication*, however, hymnologists appear to agree that the piece initially reached the printed page in Lyte's *Remains* (1850). In the end, however, the inquisitive mind can only survey a menu of choices from which

---

[7] See Genesis 29:19--"And Laban said [to Jacob], It is better that I give her [his daughter Rachel] to thee, than I should give her to another man: abide with me." (KJV)

[8] John M. Barkley (ed.), *Handbook to the Church Hymnary*, 3rd ed. (London and Oxford: Oxford University Press, 1979): 214.

[9] See, for example, "1997 Hymnodic Anniversaries," *The Hymn: A Journal of Congregational Song*, 47:4 (October 1996): 50.

to determine date and circumstances relative to the composition of this hymn. Thus, the matter remains open for anyone wishing to pursue it and end the speculation.

3. The Text As Poem

"It is an arbitrary thing, at the best," noted the American journalist, poet, and businessman Edmund Clarence Stedman (1833-1908), at the end of the nineteenth century, "to classify poets, like song-birds, into genera and species. . . . Song and hymn makers, dramatists, meditative poets, etc., are easily differentiated. . . ."[10] Song-birds and differentiations aside, the key point to Stedman's declaration focused upon his willingness to accept hymn writers as *poets*, to consider verse productions as *poetry* first and as congregational hymns second. Thus Stedman gathered no less than twenty Victorian *poets* and grouped them as "Writers of Early Hymnody": James Montgomery ("Forever with the Lord"), Charlotte Elliott ("Just as I am, without one plea"; "Let me be with thee where thou art"), James Edmeston ("Lead us heavenly Father, lead us"), Henry Hart Hilman ("When our heads are bowed with woe"; "Brother, thou art gone before us"; "Ride on! ride on, in majesty!"), John Keble ("There is a book, who runs may read"; "Lord, in thy name thy servants plead"; "The voice that breath'd o'er Eden"), Sir John Bowring ("From the recesses of a lowly spirit"), Henry Francis Lyte ("Abide with me! Fast falls the eventide"; "Jesus, I my cross have taken"; "There is a safe and secret place"), Samuel Wilberforce ("Lord, for tomorrow and its needs, I do not pray"), Christopher Wordsworth ("O Lord of heaven, and earth, and sea"), Horatius Bonar ("I was a wandering sheep"'; "I heard the voice of Jesus say"; 'T is evening now!"; "In the still air the music lies unheard"; "Beyond the smiling and the weeping I shall be soon"), John Samuel

---

[10] Stedman, *Victorian Anthology*, x.

Bewley Monsell ("When my feet have wonder'd"), William Frederick Faber ("I worship thee, sweet will of God"; "O Paradise, O Paradise"; "Oh, it is hard to work for God"), Arthur Penrhyn Stanley ("Where shall we learn to die?"), Christopher Newman Hall ("My times are in thy hand"), Anne Bronte ("My God, oh, let me call thee mine"), William John Blew ("O Lord, thy wing outspread"), Cecil Francis Alexander ("There is a green hill far away"), Elizabeth Cecelia Clephane ("There were ninety and nine that safely lay"), Sabine Baring-Gould ("Now the day is over"), and Frances Ridley Havergal ("I gave my life for thee").[11]

Note, however, the degrees to which Stedman's notion of the hymn-as-poem underwent change during the century that followed. For example, the Hunter College Professor of English, Hoxie Neale Fairchild, in his masterful six-volume study of religion in English poetry from 1700 to 1965 declared immediately that "I do not concern myself with writers whose religious verse consists wholly of hymns or psalm-paraphrases for congregational singing; but the hymns of men like [Isaac] Watts who also compose other forms of religious poetry, receive *some*[12] attention with the rest of their work."[13] Fifteen years after that, with the publication of a twelve-hundred-page anthology of Victorian literature, the editors of that volume could find room only for an indirect mention of the name of Anne Bronte, and, to the surprise of no one, that reference directed the reader to her slim reputation as a writer of fiction.[14] Finally, the publication, in 1987, of Christopher Ricks' Victorian poetry anthology set forth, as one of its features, the total exclusion of Stedman's cadre of hymnodic poets.[15] Upon

---

[11] Stedman, *Victorian Anthology*, 168-183.
[12] My italics.
[13] Hoxie Neale Fairchild, *Religious Trends in English Poetry* (New York: Columbia University Press, 1939-1968), 1:xi.
[14] John Wilson Bowyer and John Lee Brooks, *The Victorian Age: Prose, Poetry, and Drama*, 2nd ed. (New York: Appleton-Century-Crofts, 1954): 23.
[15] Christopher Ricks, *The New Oxford Book of Victorian Verse* (Oxford and New York: Oxford

reflection, the disappearance of Stedman's "twenty" from the ranks of Victorian men and women of letters might well have been the result of later editors' and critical commentators' total disregard of the hymn as a work of religious poetry or, equally, the serious decline in the *literary* quality of English hymnody during the twentieth century that left the efforts of the hymnodic *literati* of the Victorian Age totally forgotten. More importantly, however, the disappearance, or exclusion, of Stedman's "twenty" from the purely literary milieu forces one to conclude that the English hymn really needs to be considered, critically and analytically, *outside* of the traditional boundaries of English literature and within the borders of its own sovereign literary state. The hymn, announced the American hymnologist Louis Fitzgerald Benson, more than eight decades ago, "belongs among the things of the spirit, and. . .hymnody is essentially a spiritual function. The hymn is a melody in the individual heart: hymnody is the harmony of brotherhood."[16]

Having accepted that, the question then arises as to why one might even wish to consider, beyond is congregational function and service, Henry Francis Lyte's "Abide with me" as a poem. One response might be found in a critical reaction to Isaac Watts' *Horae Lyricae* (1706), in which the writers focus upon the point that the Dissenting divine proved himself "a resourceful and ambitious metrist. He set insoluble problems for himself and did not solve them completely; no poem [in that collection] is satisfactory throughout as poetry, though there are brilliant spots."[17]

Metre and metrical problems aside, the notion of "brilliant spots" in hymnodic verse might comfortably apply to Lyte's "Abide with me." For

---

University Press, 1987).
[16] Louis Fitzgerald Benson, *The Hymnody of the Christian Church* (New York: George H. Doran and Company, 1927; rpt. Richmond, Virginia: John Knox Press, 1956): vi.
[17] Martha Wynburn England and John Sparrow, *Hymns Unbidden: Donne, Herbert, Blake, Emily Dickinson, and the Hymnographers* (New York: The New York Public Library/Astor, Lennox and Tilden Foundation, 1966): 128-129.

example, the opening lines of the initial verse might appear, on the surface, as but a sensitive observation of the transition from daylight to evening and on into the darkness of the deepest recesses of the night. However, the darkness not only increases, it *thickens*. It encompasses not only the body, but it infiltrates the mind and the spirit as well; it announces the arrival of a level of spiritual depression that, particularly in the nineteenth century, can best find relief in death. Whatever else might arise as available to calm the fears, to ease the depression, to elevate the spirits, has failed; in desperation the speaker cries out for the "Help of the helpless"; he gets down upon his knees and cries out for God! Each succeeding verse increases emotionally with the intensity of the speaker's depression and fear: from "Earth's joys grow dim, its glories pass away,/Change and decay in all around I see" to the realization that "I need Thy presence every passing hour. . . ." Although the speaker's life-long struggle to commit himself to God has been sporadic, he holds sufficient reserve in his reservoir of faith to believe that "Thou hast not left me, oft as I left Thee," and thus, "On to the close, O Lord, abide with me!" If the poem does not end with a resolution to satisfy either speaker or reader, at least it closes on a note of hope:

> Hold, then, Thy Cross before my closing eyes;
>
> Speak through the gloom and point me to the skies;
>
> Heav'n's morning breaks, and earth's vain shadows flee;
>
> In life, in death, O Lord, abide with me.

The darkness has changed to light; the darkness of depression and the fear of death--or, at least, of a death without God--have been eradicated with the hope of a new life under the light of heaven.

In the end, Lyte's eight verses, as a poem, comprise a concise account of a spiritual and psychological struggle. In that regard, when viewed in its totality, without the commission of editorial surgery upon its length and alterations to its language, that poem transcends its always welcome place upon the agenda of a

Sunday morning liturgical exercise. Its clarity of thought and the poet's respect form the formalities of language truly represent what has come to be known as the literary movement within the English hymnody of the first half of the Victorian Age.

4. The Text as a Congregational Hymn

In observing and analyzing "Lyte's "Abide with me" purely as a congregational hymn, hymnologists have not always been quick to agree as to the most accurate hymnodic category under which it should be placed. Is it an evening hymn? Or, does it belong to that group of hymns to be treated as a prayer at the bedside of the dying? Does it belong, most properly, as a hymn following death, as a part of the graveside ritual? In 1881, the hymnodist and hymnologist Rev. John Ellerton (1826-1893), then rector of White Roding, Essex, produced a volume of *Notes and Illustrations of Church Hymns*, and therein he offered his comments upon this very issue. For Ellerton, Lyte's hymn "is sometimes (nearly always) classed among evening hymns, apparently on the ground of the first two lines in Keble's 'Sun of my soul.'" For the benefit of the non-specialists, the opening lines of the abbreviated (and what has become the most accepted) version of the "Evening Hymn" (1827)[18] of John Keble (1792-1866),[19] eventually among the leaders of the Oxford Movement within the Church of England, reads, "Sun of my soul, Thou Saviour dear,/It is not night if Thou be near:" In Ellerton's view--and with an extremely courteous slap upon the wrists of certain hymnal editors that might well have befitted his calling-- "This is a curious instance of the

---

[18] Published in Keble's *The Christian Year, or, Thoughts in Verse for the Sundays and Holy Days throughout the Year* (1827).
[19] A native of Fairford, Gloucestershire, and the son of a Church of England vicar, Keble received his education at Corpus Christi College, Oxford, then spent nine years as a tutor and examiner there. He left Oxford in 1823 and spent the next thirteen years as a curate in Gloucestershire. He became vicar of Hursley, near Winchester, in 1833, and in that same year received the appointment as Professor of Poetry at Oxford University.

misapprehension of the true meaning of a hymn by those among whom it is popular; for a very little consideration will suffice to show that there is not throughout the hymn the slightest allusion to the close of a natural day." One might interrupt Ellerton's narrative, at this point, in an attempt to discern the reasoning behind that divine's interpretation of Lyte's opening lines. For him, the "eventide" (the time of evening) "fast falls" (quickly "approaches," perhaps, but not yet completed), and the "darkness thickens" (or "deepens," in the majority of altered versions), but the second line relates to a spiritual state rather than the end of the light of a day. With that Rev. Professor John Barkley would agree, asserting that "Abide with me" "was not meant to be an evening hymn; its outlook is on the closing day of life."[20] Continuing, Ellerton declared that "The words of St. Luke 24:29[21] are obviously used in a sense wholly metaphorical. It [Lyte's hymn] is far better adapted to be sung at funerals, as it was beside the grave of Professor Maurice;[22] but it is almost too intense and personal for ordinary congregational use."[23] As a relevant and prophetic aside to Ellerton's final comment, one might take notice of the fact that "Abide with me" became the hymn of choice at the funeral services of a choice number of American dignitaries--among them U.S.

---

[20] Barkley, *Handbook to the Church Hymnary*, 214.

[21] "But they constrained him, saying, Abide with us: for it is toward evening, and the day is far spent. And he went in to tarry with them." (KJV)

[22] John Frederick Denison Maurice (1805-1872), English theologian and the principal founder of Christian Socialism, the son of a Unitarian minister at Normaston, near Lowestoft, Suffolk, studied at Trinity College and Trinity Hall, Cambridge, but, as a religious Dissenter, he had to leave the University in 1827 without a degree. However, he managed to undergo ordination as priest of the Church of England in 1834, then, at London, became chaplain at Guy's Hospital (1837) and at Lincoln's Inn (1841-1860). Following the publication of his one and only novel, *Eustace Conway* (1834), Maurice received the appointment of Professor of English Literature and History at King's College, London, in 1840, and in 1846 advanced to the chair of theology there. However, the University deprived him of his theology position in 1853 for alleged expressions of unorthodoxy in his *Theological Essays* (1853), concerned with atonement and eternal life. Maurice had helped to found Queen's College for Women, London (1848), as well as the Working Men's College (1854), and in 1866 he received appointment to the professorship of moral philosophy at Cambridge University. His principal works include *The Religions of the World and Their Relations to Christianity* (1847); *Moral and Metaphysical Philosophy* (1848); *The Doctrine of Sacrifice* (1854); *Social Morality* (1869). See *DNB*.

[23] Julian, *Dictionary of Hymnology*, 1:7; Duhle, *Library of Christian Hymns*, 3:751.

Senator Henry Styles Bridges of New Hampshire, at the State House, Concord, New Hampshire, on 28 November 1961; General of the Army Douglas MacArthur, at the Capitol, Washington, D.C., 9 April 1964; President Herbert Clark Hoover, at the Capitol, Washington, D.C., 25 October 1964; Governor/Ambassador Adlai Ewing Stevenson, at the National Cathedral, Washington, D.C., 15 July 1965.[24]

At any rate, although Ellerton might have set forth a reasonable argument for "Abide with me" as a funeral hymn or as one to be sung by those in mourning, he proved to have committed one error in judgment about the piece having been "too intense and personal" for an "ordinary" congregational worship service. Its continuing acceptance by a wide variety of Protestant congregations in both Great Britain and in North America has fairly well negated such critical observation.

While on the subject of hymnodic "popularity," in 1947, the World Student Christian Federation issued the fifth edition of its *Cantate Domino* (first published in 1924), containing ninety-five hymns: twenty-two in English, sixteen in German, thirteen in French, and forty-four in "other" languages. Although not all of the twenty-two English selections might be identified as among the "masterpieces" of English hymnody, they obviously merited inclusion into *Cantate Domino* because of their universal familiarity, their ease in translation,[25] and their having sounded notes of personal religious optimism and strong belief in the Church. Lyte's "Abide with me" joined such hymnodic pieces as John Greenleaf Whittier's "Dear Lord and Father of mankind"; Isaac Watts' "O God our help in ages past"; Samuel John Stone's "The Church's one foundation."[26]

---

[24] See Samuel J. Rogal, "A Survey of Hymns in Funeral Services for American Dignitaries, 1921-1969," *The Hymn: A Journal of Congregational Song*, 45:3 (July 1994):13.
[25] For example, Gustav Jensen translated five stanzas of "Abide with me" into Norwegian ("O bliv hos mig! Nu er det aftentid") for his *Forslag til Revidert Salmebok for Den Norske Kirke* (1915). For that text, see Dahle, *Library of Christian Hymns*, 3:751.
[26] Cecil Northcott, *Hymns in Christian Worship: The Use of Hymns in the Life of the Church* (Richmond, Virginia: John Knox Press, 1964): 64-65.

Two decades later, Cecil Northcott, the editorial secretary for the United Society for Christian Literature, wrote of a "charmed circle" or "sacred ring" of congregational hymns--based, naturally enough, upon a survey of hymnals-- "which is well nigh impossible to break into, and this fortress has many bastions to help defend it." The top three of Northcott's "top ten" consisted, then, of Charles Wesley's "Jesus Lover of my soul"; Henry Francis Lyte's "Abide with me"; and Isaac Watts' "When I survey the wondrous Cross."[27]

Three additional surveys of more recent vintage should be noticed. In 1994, Rev. Peter Harvey, a retired Church of England priest, solicited and collected 13,000 ballots cast by clergy, readers, churchwardens, organists, and church choir members who expressed their preferences for the most popular among hymns written during the Victorian Age. "Abide with me" ranked *seventh*. In that same year, the editors of the *Anglican Digest*, reportedly the most widely read publication within the Protestant Episcopal Church of the United States, surveyed three thousand of its readers to determine their most popular hymn. The results (published in *Anglican Digest*, 36:4 [1994]:6) found "Abide with me" at the head of the list. Then, a year later, the British Broadcasting Corporation (BBC) conducted a poll in which they asked listeners to submit the names of three of their most favorite hymns. The response of 8500 persons succeeded in placing "Abide with me" in fourth position overall.[28]

Finally, in May 1998, Professor Stephen Marini (Religion, Wellesley College), principal researcher for the American Protestant Hymn Project, released the preliminary results of a survey of 175 "historic" American hymnals and tune books in which he had ranked hymns by their frequency of inclusion in those books. Lyte's "Abide with me," having been found in eighty-five (or 48.6%) of

---

[27] Northcott, *Hymns in Christian Worship*, 76-77.
[28] Ian Bradley, *Abide With Me: The World of Victorian Hymns* (London: SCM Press Limited, 1997): 231

the volumes surveyed, ranked thirty-second among the "top" 267 hymns.[29]

Although Professor Horton Davies (History of Christianity, Princeton) did not engage in the polling/statistics game, he did set forth a number of reasonable assumptions relative to English hymnody during the Victorian Age. He viewed the period as "distinguished for the quiet spirituality of its worship, as befitted Christians engaged in troubled heart-searchings. The trumpets of the pulpits, in most cases, gave forth an uncertain sound. It was only in the realm of praise that the accents of the century are heard with unmistakable clarity, and often with poignancy." Davies then directed his discussion to John Henry Newman's "Lead, kindly Light, amid th' encircling gloom" (1833), which he identified as "both the record of a personal crisis and also typical of the epoch in its record of a struggle, its plea for Divine guidance in a darkness that makes men stumble, and its resignation." From Newman, who eventually left the Church of England for Roman Catholicism, Davies stepped immediately over to what he termed "the other most famous Victorian hymn," the keynote of nineteenth-century evangelical thought, "Abide with me, fast falls the eventide," by the Church of England country cleric Lyte. That piece, Davies maintained, "expresses the same mood, uses the inevitable image of light in darkness as it turns from the 'change and decay in all around I see' to 'O Thou who changest not, abide with me.'"[30]

Among the principal elements of the congregational hymn, the extent of the hymnodist's attention to Holy Scriptures has always been considered a matter of importance--particularly to the clergy, who remain responsible for the selection of hymns for the worship service. We have already observed John Ellerton's interpretation of the connection between the opening line of Lyte's hymn, "Abide

---

[29] Presented at the Conference on Hymnody in American Protestantism, Wheaton (IL) College, 17-20 May 2000. The American Protestant Hymns Project called for a final survey of 225 "historic" American hymnals and tune books.
[30] Horton Davies, *Worship and Theology in England. IV. From Newman to Martineau (1850-1900)* (Princeton, New Jersey: Princeton University Press, 1962; rpt. Grand Rapids, Michigan: William B. Eerdmans Publishing Company, 1996) :206.

with me; fast falls the eventide" and Luke 24:29 as "wholly metaphorical," but we may also want to re-visit that small portion within the Gospel account of the Resurrection, beginning with the verse preceding it: "And as they [the disciples and Christ] drew nigh into the village, whether they went: and he [Christ] made as though he would have gone further./But they constrained him, saying, Abide with us: for it is toward evening, and the day is far spent. And he went in to tarry with them." (KJV) Clearly, readers would have to agree with Ellerton's assessment, particularly as Lyte had shifted the language of the Gospel from "Abide with **us**" to "Abide with **me**." The second line, as well, reads "Lord, with **me** abide." The sound and the sense of the phrase "Abide with us" in the Gospel of John represent a formal request; the opening words of Lyte's hymn assume a personal plea--and an urgent one at that. In other words, "Abide with me" becomes an *evening* hymn only when one stops reading or singing it after the very first line!

In addition to its opening line, at least one-third of Lyte's hymn can be anchored, tightly or loosely, to various parts of Holy Scriptures, thus proving the piece attractive to hymnal editors who seek hymns that provide a broad congregational function within the worship service. For instance--

1:2--*The darkness thickens; Lord with me abide!*

Exodus 10:22--And Moses stretched forth his hand toward heaven; and there was a thick darkness in all the land of Egypt three days. . . .

Exodus 20:21--And the people stood far off, and Moses drew near unto the thick darkness where God was.

Deuteronomy 4:11--And ye came near and stood under the mountain; and the mountain burned with fire unto the midst of heaven, with darkness, clouds, and thick darkness.

2:3--*Change and decay in all around I see.* . . .

Leviticus 25:35--And if thy brother be waxen poor, and fallen in decay with thee, then thou shalt relieve him: ye, though he be a stranger or a sojourner; that he may live with thee.

2:4--*O Thou who changest not, abide with me.*

Psalms 15:4--In whose eyes a vile person is contemned; but he honoureth them that fear the Lord. He that sweareth to his own hurt, and changeth not.

3:4--*Come not to sojourn, but abide with me.*

Lamentations 4:15--They cried unto them, Depart ye; it is unclean; depart, depart, touch not: when they fled away and wandered, they said among the heathens, They shall no more sojourn there.

4:1--*Come not in terrors as the King of Kings. . . .*

Jeremiah 17:17--Be not in terror unto me: thou art my hope in the day of evil.

4:2--*But kind and good, with healing in Thy wings. . . .*

Malachi 4:2--But unto you that fear my name shall the Sun of righteousness arise with healings in his wings; and ye shall go forth, and grow up as calves for the stall.

4:4--*Come, friend of sinners, and thus bide with me.*

Matthew 11:19; Luke 7:34--The Son of man came eating and drinking, and they say, Behold a man gluttonous, and a winebibber, a friend of publicans and sinners. But wisdom is justified of her children.

5:4--*On to the close, O Lord, abide with me!*

Psalms 61:7--He shall abide before God forever: O prepare mercy and truth, which may preserve him.

7:3--*Where is death's sting? where, grave, Thy victory?*

1 Corinthians 15:55--O death, where is thy sing? O grave, where is thy victory?

7:4--*In triumph still, if Thou abide with me.*

Psalms 92:4--For thou, Lord, hast made me glad through thy work:

I will triumph in the works of thy hands. (KJV)

Certainly one might find additional instances of Scriptural influence upon the sound and the sense of this piece. In the end, though, the placement of Lyte's text beside Scriptures and the middle road traversed a century ago by editors of *Hymns Ancient and Modern* continue to hold true for worshipers of the present moment: "Abide with me," for that group of English hymnologists, "is commonly used as an evening hymn, but it is even more appropriate as a prayer of preparation for death, as the author intended it to be."[31] In other words, what the author *intended* to be, *shall* be!

5. The Text in Hymn Book and Hymnal

In England, the initial autograph of Lyte's "Abide with me" reached the printed page in a leaflet, generated from Berryhead, Devonshire, in September 1847; from there it went into Lyte's *Remains* (London, 1850); and, finally, became housed within his posthumously published collection, *Miscellaneous Poems* (1868). Further, in 1868, J. Wright and Company, Thomas Street, Bristol, produced a version of the piece separately, imprinted with the poet's original hymn tune.[32] Hymnal editors in the United States proved quick to include the piece in their collections, beginning with Frederick Henry Hedge's *Hymns for the Church of Christ* (Boston: Crosby, Nichols, and Company, 1853); Chandler Robbins' *Hymn Book for Christian Worship* (New York: Crosby, Nichols, and Company, 1854); and Henry Ward Beecher's *Plymouth Collection of Hymns and Tunes for the Use of Christian Congregations* (New York: A.S. Barnes, 1855). Indeed, between 1853 and 1978, "Abide with me" appeared in no less than 1349

---

[31] *Hymns Ancient and Modern* (1909), 30. One should note, however, that atop this very page of the Historical Edition of *Hymns Ancient and Modern* reads, in bold type, EVENING.

[32] Julian, *Dictionary of Hymnology*, 1:7.

American hymn books and hymnals.[33]

When the editors of the original edition of *Hymns Ancient and Modern* (1861) determined to include "Abide with me," they reasoned, rightly, that eight stanzas might exceed the vocal capacities of nineteenth-century British congregants, and so they settled upon stanzas 1, 2, 6, 7, and 8 of the original 1847 draft, with four changes in the language (indicated below in **bold**):

1 [1]   Abide with me; fast falls the eventide,
          The darkness **deepens**; Lord, with me abide;   [thickens]
          When other helpers fail, and comforts flee,
          Help of the helpless, O abide with me.

2 [2]   Swift to its close ebbs out life's little day;
          Earth's joys grow dim, its glories pass away;
          Change and decay in all around I see;
          O Thou who changest not, abide with me.

3 [6]   I need Thy presence every passing hour;
          What but Thy grace can foil the tempter's power?
          Who like Thyself my guide and stay can be?
          Through cloud and sunshine, Lord, **abide** with me!   [O abide]

4 [7]   I fear no foe with Thee at hand to bless;
          Ills have no weight, and tears no bitterness;
          Where is death's sting? where, grave, Thy victory?
          I triumph still, if Thou abide with me.

5 [8]   Hold **Thou**, Thy Cross before my closing eyes;   [then]
          Shine through the gloom and point me to the skies;   [Speak]
          Heav'n's morning breaks, and earth's vain shadows flee;

---

[33] *Dictionary of North American Hymnology. A Comprehensive Bibliography and Master Index of Hymns and Hymnals Published in the United States and Canada, 1640-1978*, comp. Leonard Ellinwood and Elizabeth Lockwood, ed. Paul R. Powell and Mary Louise Van Dyke (Boston: The Hymn Society of the United States and Canada, 2003): CD-ROM for Windows and Macintosh.

In life, in death, O Lord, abide with me.[34]

The change from *thickens* to *deepens* had been executed in the 1847 Berryhead leaflet and in the text that appeared in the 1850 *Remains*. Also in the *Remains*, "Hold *then* Thy cross" had been changed to "Hold *there*," then changed again in the 1868 collection of Lyte's *Miscellaneous Poems* to "Hold *Thou* Thy cross."[35] Regardless of those earlier language shifts and the reasoning behind them, Lyte's conception of a *thickening* darkness clearly points to the speaker's agitated state of mind and spirit; the change to *deepens* appears appropriate enough if the editors had determined (which, apparently, they did) to present Lyte's lines as purely an evening hymn; the change from the original *then* to *Thou* (5:1) emphasizes repetition over transition; and *Shine* for *Speak* in 5:2, although it illustrates, simply, the natural phenomenon from darkness to light, nonetheless removes the final plea on the part of the speaker for direct assistance from God. Finally, the omission of stanzas 3, 4, and 5 by the editors of *Hymns Ancient and Modern* from the original text eliminates the highly personal elements within the poem, particularly in stanza 5:

> Thou on my head in early youth did smile:
> And, though rebellious and perverse meanwhile,
> Thou hast not left me, oft as I left Thee,
> On to the close, O Lord, abide with me!

A century and a half later, little has changed, apparently, for certain North American hymnal editors, as close examinations of "Abide with me" in the *African American Heritage Hymnal* (Chicago: GIA Publications, Inc, 2001); *Sing to the Lord Hymnal* (Kansas City, Missouri: Lillenas Publishing Company, 1993); and *The Harvard University Hymn Book*, 4th ed., ed. Peter J. Gomes, *et al* (Cambridge, Massachusetts, and London: Harvard University Press, 2007) reveal

---

[34] *Hymns Ancient and Modern* (1909), 30.
[35] See Julian, *Dictionary of Hymnology*

the same texts (length and language) as found in *Hymns Ancient and Modern* (both 1861 and 1909 editions). *The Book of Praise* (n.p.: The Presbyterian Church in Canada, 1997) had also published the same version, with the none too surprising exception that it offered the piece in both English and French.

A number of examples of earlier hymn texts of "Abide with me" in American hymnals reveal insignificant variations--or no variations at all--from the texts in *Hymns Ancient and Modern*. The *Hymnal of the Methodist Episcopal Church. With Tunes* (New York: Nelson and Phillips, 1878), for example, exhibited the identical five stanzas and the identical four changes to the texts as found in the 1861 *Hymns Ancient and Modern*--as did the *Hymnal and Liturgies of the Moravian Church (Unitas Fratrum)* (Bethlehem, Pennsylvania: Published by Authority of the Provincial Synod, 1920); *The Hymnal. Published by Authority of the General Assembly of the Presbyterian Church in the United States of America* (Philadelphia: Presbyterian Board of Christian Education, 1933); *The Methodist Hymnal. Official Hymnal, The Methodist Episcopal Church, The Methodist Episcopal Church South, The Methodist Protestant Church* (New York, Cincinnati, Chicago: The Methodist Book Concern, 1935); *The Hymnal. Containing Complete Orders of Worship. Authorized by the General Synod of the Evangelical and Reformed Church* (St. Louis: Eden Publishing House, 1941).

However, not all American hymnal editors fell into lockstep with the *Hymns Ancient and Modern* version, and thus one can uncover a number of variations, particularly in terms of length, upon the 1861-1909 texts. The full eight stanzas will be found in the *Church Book, for the Use of Evangelical Lutheran Congregations. By Authority of the General Council of the Evangelical Lutheran Church in America* (Philadelphia: J.K. Shryock, 1897); the *Evangelical Lutheran Hymnal. Published by Order of the Evangelical Lutheran Joint Synod of Ohio and Other States*, 9th ed. (Columbus, Ohio: The Lutheran Book Concern, n.d. [1910?]; and *The Lutheran Hymnal. Authorized by the Synods Constituting the Evangelical Lutheran Synodical Conference of North America* (St. Louis: Concordia Publishing House, 1941). The editors of *Gospel Hymns Nos. 1 to 6. Excelsior Edition* (New York and Chicago: The Biglow and Main Company; Cincinnati, New York, and Chicago: the John Church Company, 1895); *The National Baptist Hymn Book: A Collection of Old Meter Songs*, 4th ed. (Nashville: National Baptist Publishing Board, 1906); and *The Broadman Hymnal: Great Standard Hymns and Choice Gospel Songs New and Old* (Nashville: The Broadman Press, 1940) included four stanzas--1, 2, 6, and 8-- from the 1847 text, while the version in the *Christian Science Hymnal* (Boston; The Christian Science Publishing Society, 1932) houses only three of the original eight stanzas--1, 6, and 7. However, the editors of this book included an additional three-stanza version of "Abide with me," this one with a text sartorially bedecked by one Bertha H. Woods, obviously intent on clothing Lyte's text in Christian Science apparel:

> 1 Abide with me; fast breaks the morning light;
> Our day-star rises, banishing all night;
> Thou art our strength, O Truth that maketh free,
> We would unfailingly abide in Thee.
>
> 2 I know no fear, with Thee at hand to bless,
> Sin hath no power and life no wretchedness;
> Health, hope and love in all around I see
> For those who trustingly abide in Thee.
>
> 3 I know Thy presence every passing hour,
> I know Thy peace, for Thou alone art power;
> O Love divine, abiding constantly,
> I need not plead, Thou dost abide with me.

The litany of editorial marchers--both in and out of step--might well continue for a number of pages, but within the last two decades, the five-stanza version appears to have become standard hymnodic fare as the principal representative of Lyte's original eight-stanza text.

6. Henry Francis Lyte (1793-1847): His Life

Born at Ednam, near Kelso, Roxburghshire, Scotland, on 1 June 1793, the second son of Captain Thomas Lyte, young Lyte initially received his formal education at Portora--formally the Royal School of Enniskillen--in County Fermanagh, Ireland.[36] From there he removed to Trinity College, Dublin (B.A. 1814), initially intent upon pursuing medical studies, becoming a scholar of that institution in 1813, and competing successfully for three prize poems within three successive years. However, he turned away from the pursuit of medicine and, instead, entered into Holy Orders of the Established Church of Ireland, and in 1815 received the appointment as curate of Taghmon, near Wexford. Ill health forced Lyte to resign his curacy and to embark upon a tour of the Continent. Following that excursion, he returned to Ireland and then, in 1817, settled into a curacy at Marazion, Cornwall. There he met and married Anne Maxwell, the daughter and eventual heiress of the then widowed Rev. William Maxwell, D.D. (1731-1818) of Falkland, County Monaghan, Ireland, and his wife, Anne Massingberd Maxwell (?-1789).

A social friend of Samuel Johnson (1709-1784), Maxwell had met the London sage in 1754, when the former served as a reader, or assistant minister, of the Temple Church, London.[37] Apparently, Maxwell had collected a number of

---

[36] Located on a hill west of the town of Enniskellen, Portora's historians can identify several dates of origin. The foundation originates from 1618, although there exist claims to a founding by James I n 1608 and later by Charles I in 1626. The present building came into existence in 1777. The Irish playwright, novelist, and poet, Samuel Barclay Beckett (1906-1989), attended Portora from 1920 to 1925). See Brendan Lehane, *A Companion Guide to Ireland*, rev. ed. (London: Collins, 1985): 390.

[37] *The Letters of Samuel Johnson*, ed. Bruce Redford (Princeton, New Jersey: Princeton University Press, 1982-1984), 1:268; 4:146; James Boswell, *Life of Samuel Johnson, LL.D.*, ed. R.W. Chapman, new ed. corr. by J.D. Fleeman (London and New York: Oxford University Press, 1970):

Johnson's comments, observations, and criticisms in his notebooks, and he had maintained a steady correspondence with Johnson following his removal to Ireland. Although a portion of those notes, as well as the correspondence, had been lost when a ship carrying that material had been raided by the American privateer John Paul Jones (1747-1792), Maxwell had managed to retrieve several of the packets, and those he sent to James Boswell in the spring of 1787 for inclusion into the latter's biography of Johnson (1791). Maxwell followed with additional notes, sent to Boswell in May 1793.[38] Although the Johnson-Boswell-Maxwell relationship predates by decades Lyte's entrance into the Maxwell family circle, one wonders, nonetheless, if William Maxwell had sufficient life remaining to exercise any literary influence over his son-in-law--or, indeed, if a significant relationship between the two ever existed. Frankly, accurate and specific dates relative to Lyte's early life prove hard to obtain.

After leaving Marazion, Lyte subsequently held curacies at Lymington, Hampshire (1819), where he composed a large portion of his verse, and of Charleton, Devonshire; and Dittisham, Devonshire. In 1822, he removed to the perpetual curacy of Lower Brixham, Devonshire, where he served for the remaining quarter-century of his life--although he had to undergo frequent foreign tours because of his poor health (most likely consumption of the lungs). Reportedly, when Lyte learned that the climate of his parish would eventually prove fatal to him if he did not relocate, he responded, "I hope not, for I know no divorce I should more deprecate than from the ocean. From childhood it has been my friend and playmate, and I have never been weary of gazing on its glorious face."[39] Nonetheless, he did depart from Cornwall, and death came to him on 20

434-449.
[38] Adam Sisman, *Boswell's Presumptuous Task: The Making of the Life of Dr. Johnson* (New York: Farrar, Straus and Giroux, 2000): 175, 276.
[39] Welsh and Edwards, *Romance of Psalter and Hymnal*, 164.

November 1847, at Nice, France, with burial in the English cemetery there. In both his personal life and clerical career, Lyte has been viewed as "a poet and a musician. . . [a] hard working curate [who] was a man of frail physique, with a face of almost feminine beauty, and a spirit as pure and gentle as a little child's."[40]

With the assistance of his son, J.W. Maxwell Lyte, Henry Francis Lyte gathered an extensive library, principally comprised of theological tracts and volumes of Old English poetry. The extent of that collection can be envisioned by the fact that its sale, in 1848, extended over a period of seventeen days. His literary career, aside from the hymns, began with two secular poems, "On a Naval Officer" and "The Poet's Plea"-- the first cited title having been set to music by Sir Arthur Seymour Sullivan (1842-1900). His published volumes of verse begin with *Tales in Verse* (1826), written and assembled during his clerical tenure at Lymington and followed by a second edition; the Scottish literary critic John Wilson (1785-1854)--writing in the series of dialogues, "Noctes Ambrosianae," as "Christopher North" for *Blackwood's Edinburgh Magazine*--characterized Lyte's verse as "the right kind of religious poetry." His *Poems Chiefly Religious* reached a London press in 1833, with a second edition in 1845--the latter reprinted in 1868 as *Miscellaneous Poems*--while we have already noted the volume of *Remains* (1850), consisting of poems, sermons and letters. Finally, one should note his "Biographical Sketch of Henry Vaughan [1622-1695]," prefixed within his edition of the British mystic poet's *Sacred Poems* (London: Pickering, 1847; rpt. Boston, 1854, 1856)--the first edition of a complete work of Henry Vaughan to have been published since the seventeenth century.[41] The less than minor painter John King (1788-1847) executed a portrait of Lyte (engraved by an artist named Phillips), which resides in the British Museum and appears facing page ci (101) of the

---

[40] Brown and Butterworth, *Story of the Hymns and Tunes*, 217.
[41] England and Sparrow, *Hymns Unbidden*, 1.

Historical Edition of *Hymns Ancient and Modern* (1909).[42]

7. Henry Francis Lyte: Hymnodist

The total of Lyte's hymns and psalm paraphrases that have drifted in and out of congregational hymnals and hymnbooks number no less than 105 pieces. As far as concerns numbers, one must be especially cautious in searching through mid- to late-nineteenth-century American and English hymn books and hymnals, since more than one or two editors during that period became confused by the appearance of two collections under the same title: *Spirit of the Psalms* (1829), published anonymously by Harriet Auber (1773-1862), under the guidance of an equally anonymous English clergyman, which included her own paraphrases and a small number of hymns undertaken by other hands; and Lyte's *Spirit of the Psalms* (1834; enlarged 1836)--psalm paraphrases, all of them by Lyte and published for the benefit of his own congregation at Lower Brixham--that volume becoming the principal source of his hymnodic verse available to compilers of hymn books and hymnals. Hasty and inattentive editors (and/or their assistants) simply assumed that *both* books came from Lyte's pen, and thus he has received credit for hymns actually authored by Miss Auber. For example, in *The Sabbath Hymn Book for the Service of Song in the House of the Lord* (New York: Mason Brothers; Boston, J.E. Tilton and Company, 1858), Harriet Auber's name does not even appear in the first-line index or in the index of authors of hymns; yet, the editors assigned sixteen hymns to Henry Francis Lyte, nine of those pieces actually written by Miss Auber.

That issue aside, of the approximately 105+ hymns produced by Lyte (or generated from various of his original hymns and Scripture paraphrases), only seventeen (17) have achieved degrees of consistently minimal acceptance by

---

[42] See *DNB*, 35:365-366; Barkley, *Handbook to the Church Hymnary*, 3rd ed, 303; Julian, *Dictionary of Hymnology*, 1:706-707.

congregations, and can be identified as--

>Abide with me; fast falls the eventide (1847)
>
>*Far from my heavenly home (1834)
>
>*God of mercy, God of grace (1834)
>
>Hark round the God of love (1838)
>
>Jesus, I my cross have taken (1824)[43]
>
>*Long did I toil and knew no earthly rest (1833)
>
>Loud was the wind and wild the tide 1833)
>
>O Lord how good, how great art Thou (1833)
>
>*Oh had I, my Saviour, the wings of a dove (1834)
>
>*Pleasant are Thy courts above (1834)
>
>*Praise, my soul, the King of heaven (1834)
>
>*Praise the Lord, His glories show (1834)
>
>Sing to the Lord a new-made song (1834)
>
>Sweet evening hour! Sweet evening hour! (1833)
>
>*There is a safe and secret place (1834)
>
>Thy promise, Lord, is perfect peace (1834)
>
>*When at Thy footstool, Lord, I bend (1833)

In addition, of course, to "Abide with me," of the number listed immediately preceding, nine others of them (marked [*]) have managed to cling to life as standard hymnodic fare: (1) "Far from my heavenly home," a paraphrase of Psalms 137, in five four-line stanzas; (2) "God of mercy, God of grace," a hymn of three six-line stanzas based upon Psalms 67; (3) "Long did I toil, and knew no

---

[43] This piece proved to have been one of the few of Lyte's hymnodic contributions that evidences a specific bibliographic trail of sorts. It appeared initially in *Sacred Poetry*, 3rd ed. (Edinburgh: Oliphant and Sons, 1824), in six stanzas of eight lines each, bearing the heading "Lo, we have left all and followed Thee (Matthew 19:27)" and signed "G." It appeared next in James Montgomery's *The Christian Psalmist* (1825), again signed "G," but without that signature in *The Family Visitor* (1826) and *Hymns for Private Devotion* (1827)--all of that before inclusion in Lyte's own *Poems Chiefly Religious* (1833). See Dahle, *Library of Christian Hymns*, 2:593.

earthly rest"--a mosaic of Biblical sources, including Matthew 11:28, John 15:5, Hebrews 13:8, 1 Corinthians 13:8-12; (4)"Oh, had I, my Saviour, the wings of a dove," a paraphrase of Psalms 55; (5) "Pleasant are Thy courts above," in four stanzas of eight lines each and paraphrasing Psalms 84; (6) "Praise, my soul, the King of heaven"--a paraphrase of Psalms 103 that editors have, generally, agreed to allow to remain unaltered from the original text of five six-line stanzas; (7) "Praise the Lord, His glories show," a free paraphrase of Psalms 150; (8) "There is a safe and secret place," a five-stanza paraphrase of Psalms 91:1-2; (9) "When at Thy footstool, Lord, I bend," a text based upon 1 John 2:1, in six stanzas of four lines each. Of the remainder of Lyte's hymnodic corpus, fifteen (15) hymns derive from his *Poems Chiefly Religious* (1833, 1845) and sixty-six (66) from his *Spirit of the Psalms* (1834).[44]

The critical assessment of Lyte's hymns and psalm paraphrases focuses upon their reflection of the poet's sadness, tenderness, tearfulness and beauty--all of which tend to underscore the conscientious but excessive physical labor and the pressing spiritual anxieties that contributed to the weakening of an already weakened bodily condition. Therefore, one has to reach deeply into the published volumes to uncover the few, if indeed any, texts with genuine but obviously muted notes of joy or gladness--the single exceptions, perhaps being found in "Pleasant are Thy courts above"--

> Happy birds that sing and fly
> Round Thy altars, O most High;
> Happier souls that find a rest
> In a heavenly Father's breast;
> Like the wandering dove that found
> No response on earth around,

---

[44] Julian, *Dictionary of Hymnology*, 1:706-707.

> They can to their work repair,
>
> And enjoy it ever there. (2:1-8)

Essentially, though, the echoes and the memories generating from the thin strains of Lyte's contributions to congregational hymnody clearly reflect the qualities of one person's affliction, grief, and overall unhappiness:

> Man may trouble and distress me,
>
> 'T will but drive me to Thy breast;
>
> Life with trials hard may press me,
>
> Heaven will bring me sweeter rest.
>
> O, 't is not the grief to harm me
>
> While Thy love is left to me,
>
> O, 't is not in joy to charm me
>
> Were that joy unmixed with Thee.
>
> (from "Jesus, I my cross have taken")[45]

In the last analysis, however, the name of Henry Francis Lyte will always be linked to but a single congregational hymn, "Abide with me; fast falls the eventide." No matter how hard or for how long one squeezes the tube of his total poetic substance, that one piece continues to comprise the essential matter of Lyte's contribution to English and American congregation song. Those hymns that remain appear but shadows lingering beneath the light of the one hymn with which he bid farewell to his Cornish congregation and, essentially, to his own life.

8. The Hymn Tunes and Their Composers

We have noted previously in this discussion that Lyte reportedly composed an original hymn tune for "Abide with me." If, indeed, he did, the notes and measures from that composition appear never to have wafted beyond Cornwall to

---

[45] See Julian, *Dictionary of Hymnology*, 1:707, 2:921; *Hymns Ancient and Modern* (1909), no. 389, p. 522; Brown and Butterworth, *Story of Hymns and Tunes*, 221-222.

capture the fancies of hymnal editors and congregational worshipers. Unquestionably, that tune had been swept aside into the dust heap of neglect, and Lyte's hymn lingered in a semi-obscure state for some fourteen years until the editors of *Hymns Ancient and Modern* (1861), who had begun their work as early as 1857, literally plucked the country cleric's piece from its provincial Cornish oblivion and placed it upon their own page, set to a tune by Sir William Henry Monk (1823-1889), then organist and director of the choir at King's College, London. "If "Abide with me' is a proper church hymn," lectured Louis Fitzgerald Benson to a Princeton Theological Seminary gathering in 1926, "Monk's tune is its 'proper tune.' It would be mere affectation to set it to a plainsong melody."[46] However, an extremely small number of hymnologists, musicologists, students, and scholars of the English hymn have, by now, settled themselves comfortably into recognizing the fact that Monk proved not the only musician to have set Lyte's hymn text to music. He certainly raised the piece to broad congregational acceptance and respectability, and he might well have been the first to set "Abide with me" to a meaningful and popular tune, but more so, his composition had, in turn, motivated the efforts of a number of music-minded contemporaries who, also, had been attracted to the somber text of Lyte's hymn.

If the compositions of hymn texts tend to gather anecdotal moss relative to how, when, and where they emerged from the creative womb, the origins of hymn tunes do not suffer any less from such afflictions. According to a variety of sources, Monk composed the tune for "Abide with me," known, simply and obviously enough, as "Eventide," at the close of one of the meetings occupied with the compilation of *Hymns Ancient and Modern*. From an account published in *The Musical Times* for January 1908 (p. 23), Monk required only ten minutes of his time to transfer the notes from his mind to the page--even though the sounds

---

[46] Louis F. Benson, *The Hymnody of the Christian Church* (New York: George H. Doran and Company, 1927; rpt. Richmond, Virginia: John Knox Press, 1956):264

of a nearby pianoforte lesson resounded within his musical ear. Another source agreed with the preceding, adding to it only a generous dose of rhetorical embellishment with, "In ten minutes. . .Dr. Monk composed the sweet, pleading chant that is wedded permanently to Lyte's swan song."[47] A third teller of tales introduced a narrative supposedly related by Monk, himself, to the effect that when he and Sir Henry Williams Baker (1821-1877), the principal textual editor of *Hymns Ancient and Modern,* "were once going out, they suddenly remembered that there was no tune for hymn 27, 'Abide with me,'[48] and that he sat down, and, undisturbed by the noise of a piano lesson which was then going on, wrote that excellent and popular tune in ten minutes."[49] However, Monk's widow later contradicted all such scenarios, declaring that the tune had been written by her husband in her company, out of doors and during a period of considerable (but unidentified) sorrow, both of them standing for an extended length of time and observing a strikingly beautiful sunset.[50] The moral of the story appears to be that Monk possessed the facility to compose hymn tunes in quick order.

No matter how and when Monk generated "Eventide," there arises little doubt among the majority of hymnologists and musicologists alike that in applying the tune to "Abide with me," the composer extracted from the hymn "every ounce of its writer's pathos and sentiment."[51] Certain among Monk's contemporaries, however, harbored other thoughts, and one complainant, obviously familiar with the nuances of composition and theory and intent upon demonstrating his eruditeness to the public, addressed a letter to *The Musical Record* on 30 January 1865, to the effect that in "Eventide" there exists "in bar 3 a

---

[47] Brown and Butterworth, *Story of Hymns and Tunes,* 219.
[48] An error in the "story" here: In the first edition of *Hymns Ancient and Modern,* the editors placed "Abide with me" as hymn no. 14; in the Revised Edition of 1875, they moved the piece back to hymn no. 27.
[49] Welsh and Edwards, *Romance of Psalter and* Hymnal, 314.
[50] *Hymns Ancient and Modern* (1909), 30.
[51] Bradley, *Abide with Me,* 152.

double minor seventh; in bar 5 an unresolved fourth-sixth; in bar 7 a minor seventh resolved upwards; in bar 11 a revival of the ill-sounding discord of major third and minor sixth; in bar 13 a strain commencing on a discord; and throughout the tune, wherever a discord will 'stick,' there will such be found, viz. in 16 chords out of 40."[52]

The hymnodic marriage between the text of "Abide with me" and the tune "Eventide" stands, metaphorically, as a contrast between Henry Francis Lyte, the practically obscure curate-poet from rural Cornwall, and William Henry Monk, in his day a leading London choral director and academician who proved a major influence on English congregational song. A native of the Brompton section of London, Monk pursued his formal music studies under the directions of the organist Thomas Adams (1785-1858), the piano pedagogue and music theorist James Alexander Hamilton (1785-1845), and the organist G.A. Griesbach. He then obtained positions, in London, as organist at Eaton Chapel, Pimlico; St. George's Chapel, Albemarle Street; and Portman Chapel, St. Marylebone, before receiving, in 1847, the appointment to the directorship of the choir in King's College, London, as well as becoming organist there two years later. Expanding the sphere of his interests, Monk, in 1851, became professor of music at the School for the Indigent Blind, and in the year following he accepted the appointment as organist at St. Matthias Church, Stoke Newington, London, where he also directed a volunteer choir that participated in a daily choral service. In 1874, following the resignation of John Pyke Hullah (1812-1884)--with whom he had been associated in the promotion of popular music education--Monk succeeded his colleague, Hullah, as professor of vocal music at King's College. Monk also delivered lectures on music at the London Institution (1850-1879); the Philosophical Institution, Edinburgh; and the Royal Institution, Manchester. Other

---

[52] Bradley, *Abide with Me*, 152-153, 267.

academic positions came to him in the form of professorships at the National Training School for Music (1876), and at Bedford College, London (1878).

Monk served as music editor of *The Parish Choir*, the organ of the Society for Promoting Church Music, beginning with its forty-first number in June 1849. Although a committed and outspoken traditionalist within the Church of England, he also assisted in editing the musical portions of Henry Allon's *The Congregational Psalmist* (1858), and performed the same task for the second edition of *The Scottish Hymnal: Hymns for Public Worship Selected by a Committee of the General Assembly of the Church of Scotland. Published for Use in Churches by the General Assembly* (Edinburgh: Blackwood, 1872).[53] Nevertheless, despite the sheer variety of his music activities and projects, insofar as concerns English hymnody and church music in general, Monk's reputation lies within the pages of *Hymns Ancient and Modern* (1861). In late 1859 or early 1860, Sir Henry Williams Baker (1821-1877), vicar of Monkland, Herefordshire, and secretary of the committee for the compilation of the new hymnal,[54] recommended Monk's appointment as music editor of the proposed volume; to Monk has been extended credit for bestowing the name *Hymns Ancient and Modern* upon the forthcoming book. Although Monk performed the vast portion of the work in assigning, arranging, and adapting tunes to the texts--and composing seventeen of them himself--the Reverend Sir Frederick Arthur Gore Ousley (1825-1889), organist, pianist, and Professor of Music at Oxford University (from 1855 until his death), revised tunes when necessary and eventually approved all of the music for the volume.[55]

---

[53] See Barkley, *Handbook to the Church Hymnary*, 3rd ed, 315; *ve's Dictionary of Music and Musicians*, 3rd ed., ed. H.C. Colles (New York: The Macmillan Company, 1944), 3:495; Benson. *The English Hymn*, 510, 521, 523, 535, 542.

[54] Although almost totally the work of members of the Church of England, and although an echo of Church theology, *Hymns Ancient and Modern* never received the stamp as an "official" hymnal of the Church of England.

[55] *Hymns Ancient and Modern* (1909), cv-cviii [105-108].

One question relative to Monk's "Eventide" concerns its setting to a hymn text *other* than that of Lyte's "Abide with me." In other words, does the tune exist only as a "single-hymn" piece? The answer, generally, appears to be a qualified "Yes," provided that one believes in sampling. Thus, in the following hymnals, "Eventide" belongs to no text other than "Abide with me": *Hymns Ancient and Modern* (1861, 1875); the *Church Book for the Use of Evangelical Lutheran Congregations* (1897); the *Wartburg Hymnal* (1918); *Hymnal and Liturgies of the Moravian Church* (1920); *Christian Science Hymnal* (1932); *The Hymnal. . .of the Presbyterian Church* (1933); *The Methodist Hymnal* (1935); *Services of Religion for Use in the Churches of the Free Spirit* (1937); *The Broadman Hymnal* (1940); *Christian Worship: A Hymnal* (1941); *The Hymnal. . .of the Evangelical and Reformed Church* (1941); *The Lutheran Hymnal* (1941); *New Songs of Service* (1944); *Devotional Hymns* (1947); *Church Service Hymns* (1948); *Favorite Hymns of Praise* (1967); *The Church Hymnary* (1973); *Worship His Majesty* (1987); *The United Methodist Hymnal* (1989); *The Worshiping Church* (1990); *Sing to the Lord* (1993); *The Celebration Hymnal* (1997); *The Book of Praise* (1997); the *African American Heritage Hymnal* 2001); *The Harvard University Hymn Book* (2007).

The one exception? The editors of the *Hymnal of the Methodist Episcopal Church* (1878) set Monk's "Eventide" to "Abide with me" and to John Ellerton's parting hymn of praise, "Saviour again, to Thy dear name we raise" (1866)--the opening stanza of which will, hopefully, satisfy the appetites of those who wish, at this point, to sing:

> Saviour, again to Thy dear name we raise,
> With one accord, our parting hymn of praise;
> We stand to bless Thee ere our worship cease,
> Then lowly kneeling, wait Thy word of peace. (1:1-4)

As indicated at the outset of this discussion of "Abide with me" and its musical settings, following the publication of Lyte's text and Monk's tune in *Hymns Ancient and Modern*, the piece began its ascendancy upon the ladder of hymnodic popularity, and thus attracted the collective attentions of a number of composers who resided within the broad sphere of music for the Church. Among those would have been Samuel Sebastian Wesley (1810-1876)--the eldest of the seven surviving (of at least nine) illegitimate children of Samuel Wesley the youngest (1766-1837)[56] and his mistress, Sarah Suter (1793?-1863), and thus the grandson of Charles Wesley (1707-1788) and the grand-nephew of John Wesley (1703-1791). Born at London in the initial year of his father's relationship with Sarah Suter, young Wesley, in 1820 and at age ten, entered the Chapel Royal, St. James's, London, as a chorister, and from there, still at a young age, obtained positions as organist at several London churches: St. James's, Hampstead Road (1826); St. Giles, Camberwell (1829); St. John's, Waterloo Road (1829); Hampton-on-Thames (1830). In 1832, Wesley became organist of Hereford Cathedral, where, in 1834, he conducted the Three Choirs Festival--or, formally, the Meeting of the Three Choirs of Gloucester, Winchester, and Hereford[57]-- after which he removed to Exeter Cathedral (1835-1841). At Exeter, he established his reputation as the principal organist and composer of church music in England. In 1842, Wesley accepted the position of organist at Leeds parish church, and during that period he delivered a series of lectures at the Liverpool Collegiate Institution. Then followed positions at Winchester Cathedral (1849), a professorship in organ at the Royal Academy of Music (1850), and, finally, he settled in as organist at Gloucester Cathedral (1865).[58]

Samuel Sebastian Wesley's principal contribution to congregational

---

[56] Summaries of the correspondence between Samuel Sebastian Wesley and his father will be found in Michael Kassler and Philip Oleson, *Samuel Wesley (1766-1837): A Source Book* (Aldershot, England, and Burlington, Vermont: Ashgate Publishing Limited, 2001).
[57] See *Grove's Dictionary of Music and Musicians*, 3rd ed., 5:337-339.
[58] *Grove's Dictionary of Music and Musicians*, 4th ed., 5:702-703.

hymnody came forth with the publication of his *The European Psalmist* (London: Novello, Boosey, and Hamilton, 1872)--a 558-page collection of 733 music pieces, 615 of them hymn tunes (143 of Wesley's own composition). Nestled among the leaves of this volume lie three settings to "Abide with me," two of them original, the third his arrangement of a tune known as "Reliance." The arrangement proves difficult to identify precisely, since Wesley had consulted a volume entitled *Harmonia Perfecta* (1730) and thus assigned the authorship of "Reliance" to the composer and organist Michael Wise (1648?-1687), sometime master of the choristers of St. Paul's Cathedral, London. However, the correct source of the tune would have been found in an earlier book compiled by one "W.L." and bearing the title *A Collection of Tunes* (1719). The two original tunes--nos. 559 and 580, respectively, in *The European Psalmist*--claim the names of "Orisons" (meaning "prayers") and Refuge."[59] Certainly, Wesley's three settings, as well as the entire collection that he compiled, have contributed, minimally, to the history of hymnody in England, but neither the tunes nor the volume could diminish the lights of the newly found popularity of "Abide with me" that emanated from the combination of Lyte's poetic text and Monk's music. As two nineteenth-century historians of hymnody have jointly and justly noted, "In his hymn-tunes he [Monk] possessed such power in fitting appropriate music to words that it would in many cases be almost a sacrilege to dissociate them."[60]

Proceeding quickly and rather loosely in terms of clear chronology, the musicologist and hymnologist Erik Routley claimed that Monk's "Eventide" stood, in the 1860's, as "neither the earliest tune written for the words [of "Abide with me"] nor by any general consent the inevitable one." Routley then cited the *Congregational Hymn and Tune Book* (enlarged ed., 1862), wherein the compiler,

---

[59] Erik Routley, *The Musical Wesleys* (London: Herbert Jenkins, 1968): 215-216.
[60] Welsh and Edwards, *Romance of Psalter and Hymnal*, 313.

Richard Robert Chope (1830-1910?), a Church of England curate and church choral musician, set Lyte's hymn to the tune "St. Saviour," by one R.F. Smith. Further, according to Routley's investigations, three other books of the period set "Abide with me" to the Genevan tune, "Old 124th"[61]: *The Bristol Tune Book* (1863); *Hymns for the Church of England* (1865), edited by Charles H. Steggall (1826-1905), then on the faculty of the Royal Academy of Music and organist at Lincoln's Inn Chapel, London; and *Psalms and Hymns* (1867), compiled by James Turle (1802-1882), organist and master of the choristers at Westminster Abbey, and music master at the School for the Indigent Blind, London (1829-1856)-- where he must have known William Henry Monk, who, as has been noted above, joined the faculty there in 1851. However, one should be quick to note that "Abide with me" set to those tunes identified by Routley *followed* the publication of Monk's "Eventide," and that the latter, in relatively short time, simply eclipsed those "other" efforts of the 1860's and 1870's.[62]

9. Personal Reaction

As a common denominator of sorts with books, motion picture films, Shakespearean plays, and popular songs, certain congregational hymns establish themselves as "classics" of the genre, both within and beyond the worship service, because people embrace them in the *totality* of their composition. In fiction or theatre, for example, characters become as important as plots, and in hymnody, words and music take equal hold upon the hearts and minds of singers. In cathedral stalls and in church pews, the words of the hymn must flow forth

---

[61] "Old 124th" initially appeared in the 1551 *Genevan Psalter*, set to the version of Psalms 124 by Theodorus Beza (1519-1605), the French Protestant theologian who adopted Protestantism at Geneva in 1548, became a leader of the Reformation in France, and succeeded John Calvin upon the latter's death in 1564. William Whittingham (1524?-1579), dean of Durham Cathedral from 1563, had, assisted in the translation of the Geneva Bible in 1560, and thus produced an English version of Psalms 124.

[62] See Routley, *The Musical Wesleys*, 204, 213-214.

from and upon notes; to speak the words without the notes or to hum the tune without the words simply will not suffice. As indicated above, separation of the words from the music destroys the totality of the hymn.

Unfortunately, in the congregational hymn, the words can and do easily become separated from the music, and the latter can, with greater ease, obscure the former. At the risk of a bad metaphor, music speaks louder than words! With the exceptions of trained opera soloists, vocalists, and choristers, the vast majority of the weekly (or less, mostly) visitors to their neighborhood pews have not been schooled to sing and to think simultaneously. At best, they tend to forget the written text of the hymn, but somehow retain the sounds of the music. In addition, at such rituals and ceremonies as funerals, university graduations, and the commissioning of ships, bands blare forth hymn tunes without any thoughts of encouraging or even permitting persons to sing the words. Indeed, if every offering in the hymnal could be set to such tunes as Monk's "Eventide," Stuart K. Hine's "How Great Thou Art," Arthur Seymour Sullivan's "St. Gertrude," or Henry T. Smart's "Lancashire," then the pews would likely be packed in anticipation of a spirited hymn-sing--no matter what the language or the substance of the hymns.

Professor Ian Bradley, in discussing the "continuing strong hold of Victorian hymns upon the popular imagination. . .[through] their use at public occasions," cites the example of the tradition of singing Lyte's "Abide with me" at the Football Association Cup championship finals. That practice, announced Bradley, began in 1927, when the secretary of the Association, Sir Alfred Wall, brought the matter to King George V and Queen Mary (Elizabeth II's grandparents)--both of whom harbored deep affections for the piece.[63] Certainly, although an hymnologist might appreciate the gesture, those outside that

---

[63] Bradley, *Abide With Me*, 225.

discipline might be hard pressed to see the relationship between a forthcoming soccer football match and the words of a dying country curate--unless, of course, Lyte's seventh stanza be permitted the widest possible range of critical interpretation:

> I fear no foe with Thee at hand to bless;
> Ills have no weight, and tears no bitterness;
> Where is death's sting? where, grave, Thy victory?
> I triumph still, if Thou abide with me. (7:1-4)

However, neither soccer football nor rituals, indoor or outdoor, hold the keys to those residents of the present moment achieving an understanding of, and then emotionally embracing, Lyte's hymn and Monk's hymn tune. Those who grasp the sense of its words while singing its notes do so because those eight hymn stanzas represent ideals and values and ethics that, for too long, have been fading before them. Instead, in the front ranks of human priorities, marches a phalanx of gimmicks and gadgets and trends, supported by loud language and flashing lights and quick movements and terribly bad manners. For those taken aback by--and actually fear, if you will--the hordes of a contemporary culture who appear too oblivious of their past, too ignorant of their present, and too blind to their future, there exists little else but the comfort offered within a small isthmus of the hymnodic word and world:

> Swift to its close ebbs out life's little day;
> Earth's joys grow dim, its glories pass away;
> Change and decay in all around I see;
> **O Thou who changest not, abide with me.** (2:1-4)

10. List of Words Cited and Consulted

A. Primary Sources (Texts)

Boswell, James. *The Life of Samuel Johnson, LL.D.*, ed. R.W. Chapman, new ed.

corr. by J.D. Fleeman. London and New York: Oxford University Press, 1970.

Bowyer, John Wilson, and John Lee Brooks, *The Victorian Age: Prose, Poetry, and Drama*, 2nd ed. New York: Appleton-Century-Crofts, 1954.

The Letters of Samuel Johnson, ed. Bruce Redford. 5 vols. Princeton, New Jersey: Princeton University Press, 1982-1984.

Ricks, Christopher, ed. *The New Oxford Book of Victorian Verse..* Oxford and New York: Oxford University Press, 1987.

Stedman, Edmund Clarence, ed. *A Victorian Anthology (1837-1895). Selections Illustrating the Editor's Critical Review of British Poetry in the Reign of Victoria.* Boston and New York: Houghton, Mifflin and Company, 1896.

B. Secondary Sources

Barkley, John M., ed. *Handbook to the Church Hymnary*, 3rd ed. London and Oxford: Oxford University Press, 1979.

Benson, Louis Fitzgerald. *The Hymnody of the Christian Church.* New York: George H. Doran and Company, 1927; rpt. Richmond, Virginia: John Knox Press, 1956.

Bradley, Ian. *Abide With Me: The World of Victorian Hymns.* London: SCM Press Limited, 1997.

Brown, Theron, and Hezekiah Butterworth. *The Story of the Hymns and Tunes.* New York: American Tract Society, 1906.

Dahle, John. *Library of Christian Hymns*, trans. M. Casper Johnshoy. 3 vols. Minneapolis, Minnesota: Augsburg Publishing House, 1928.

Davies, Horton. *Worship and Theology in England. IV. From Newman to Martineau (1850-1900).* Princeton, New Jersey: Princeton University Press, 1962; rpt. Grand Rapids, Michigan: William B. Eerdmans Publishing Company, 1996.

Dictionary of National Biography (DNB).

Dictionary of North American Hymnology. A Comprehensive Bibliography and Master Index of Hymns and Hymnals Published in the United States and Canada, 1640-1978, comp. Leonard Ellinwood and Elizabeth Lockwood, ed. Paul R. Powell and Mary Louise Van Dyke. Boston: The Hymn Society of the United States and Canada, 2003. CD-ROM for Windows and Mackintosh

England, Martha Wynburn, and John Sparrow, *Hymns Unbidden: Donne, Herbert, Blake, Emily Dickinson, and the Hymnographers.* New York: The New York Public Library/Astor, Lennox and Tilden Foundation, 1966.

Fairchild, Hoxie Neale. *Religious Trends in English Poetry.* 6 vols. New York: Columbia University Press, 1939-1968.

Grove's Dictionary of Music and Musicians, 3rd ed., ed. H.C. Colles. 7 vols. New York: The Macmillan Company, 1944.

Julian, John. *A Dictionary of Hymnology,* 2nd rev. ed., with Supplement. 2 vols. London: John Murray, 1907; rpt. New York: Dover Publications, Inc., 1957.

Kassler, Michael, and Philip Oleson, *Samuel Wesley (1766-1837): A Source Book.* Aldershot, England, and Burlington, Vermont: Ashgate Publishing Limited, 2001).

Lehane, Brendan. *A Companion Guide to Ireland,* rev. ed. London: Collins, 1985.

"1997 Hymnodic Anniversaries." *The Hymn: A Journal of Congregational Song,* 47:4 (October 1996): 50.

Northcott, Cecil. *Hymns in Christian Worship: The Use of Hymns in the Life of the Church.* Richmond, Virginia: John Knox Press, 1964.

Rainbow, Bernarr. *The Choral Revival in the Anglican Church (1839-1872).* New York: Oxford University Press, 1970.

Rogal, Samuel J. "A Survey of Hymns in Funeral Services for American Dignitaries, 1921- 1969." *The Hymn: A Journal of Congregational Song,* 45:3 (July 1994):11-15.

Routley, Erik. *The Musical Wesleys.* London: Herbert Jenkins, 1968.

Sisman, Adam. *Boswell's Presumptuous Task: The Making of the Life of Dr. Johnson.* New York: Farrar, Straus and Giroux, 2000.

Welsh, R.E., and F.G. Edwards. *The Romance of Psalter and Hymnal: Authors and Composers.* London; Hodder and Stoughton, 1889.

C. Hymnals

African American Heritage Hymnal. Chicago: GIA Publications, Inc, 2001.

Beecher, Henry Ward. *Plymouth Collection of Hymns and Tunes for the Use of Christian Congregations.* New York: A.S. Barnes, 1855.

The Book of Praise. n.p.: The Presbyterian Church in Canada, 1997.

The Broadman Hymnal: Great Standard Hymns and Choice Gospel Songs New and Old. Nashville: The Broadman Press, 1940.

The Celebration Hymnal. Songs and Hymns for Worship. Containing Scriptures from the King James Version of the Holy Bible. n.p.: Word Music/Integrity Music, 1997.

Christian Science Hymnal. Boston; The Christian Science Publishing Society, 1932.

Christian Worship. A Hymnal. St. Louis: The Bethany Press, 1941.

Church Book, for the Use of Evangelical Lutheran Congregations. By Authority of the General Council of the Evangelical Lutheran Church in America. With Music, Arranged for the Use of Congregations, by Harriet Reynolds Krauth. Philadelphia: J.K. Shryock, 1897.

Church Service Hymns. A Superior Collection of Hymns and Gospel Songs, ed. Homer Rodeheaver, George W. Sanville, and B.D. Ackley. Winona Lake, Indiana: Rodeheaver Company, 1948.

Devotional Hymns. A Collection of Hymns and Songs for Use in All Services of the Church, Including Sunday School, Young People's Meetings, Missionary and Mid-Week Services. Chicago: Hope Publishing Company, 1947.

Evangelical Lutheran Hymnal. Published by Order of the Evangelical Lutheran Joint Synod of Ohio and Other States, 9th ed. Columbus, Ohio: The Lutheran Book Concern, n.d. [1910?].

Favorite Hymns of Praise. Wheaton, Illinois: Tabernacle Publishing Company, 967.

Gospel Hymns Nos. 1 to 6. Excelsior Edition, ed. Ira D. Sankey, James McGranahan, George . Stebbins, Philip P. Bliss. New York and Chicago: The Biglow and Main Company; Cincinnati, New York, and Chicago: the John Church Company, 1895.

The Harvard University Hymn Book, 4th ed., ed. Peter J. Gomes, *et al.* Cambridge, Massachusetts, and London: Harvard University Press, 2007.

Hedge, Frederick Henry. *Hymns for the Church of Christ.* Boston: Crosby, Nichols, and Company, 1853.

Hymnal and Liturgies of the Moravian Church (Unitas Fratrum). Bethlehem, Pennsylvania: Published by Authority of the Provincial Synod, 1920.

The Hymnal. Containing Complete Orders of Worship. Authorized by the General Synod of the Evangelical and Reformed Church. St. Louis: Eden Publishing House, 1941.

Hymnal of the Methodist Episcopal Church. With Tunes. New York: Nelson and Phillips, 1878.

The Hymnal. Published by Authority of the General Assembly of the Presbyterian Church in the United States of America. Philadelphia: Presbyterian Board of Christian Education, 1933.

Hymns Ancient and Modern, for Use in the Services of the Church. With

Accompanying Tunes. Historical Edition London: William Clowes and Sons, Limited, 1909.

The Lutheran Hymnal. Authorized by the Synods Constituting the Evangelical Lutheran Synodical Conference of North America. St. Louis: Concordia Publishing House, 1941.

The Methodist Hymnal. Official Hymnal, The Methodist Episcopal Church, The Methodist Episcopal Church South, The Methodist Protestant Church. New York, Cincinnati, Chicago: The Methodist Book Concern, 1935.

The National Baptist Hymn Book: A Collection of Old Meter Songs, 4th ed. Nashville: National Baptist Publishing Board, 1906.

A New Hymnal for Colleges and Schools, ed. Jeffery Rowthorn and Russell Schulz-Widmar. New Haven, Connecticut, and London, England: Yale University Press/Yale Institute of Sacred Music, 1992.

Robbins, Chandler. *Hymn Book for Christian Worship*. New York: Crosby, Nichols, and Company, 1854.

The Sabbath Hymn Book for the Service of Song in the House of the Lord, ed. Edwards Amasa Park and Austin Phelps. New York: Mason Brothers; Boston, J.E. Tilton and Company, 1858.

Services of Religion for Use in the Churches of the Free Spirit.[64] Boston: The Beacon Press, Inc., 1937.

Sing to the Lord. Hymnal. Kansas City, Missouri: Lillenas Publishing Company, 1993.

The United Methodist Hymnal. Book of United Methodist Worship. Nashville: The United Methodist Publishing House, 1989.

Wartburg Hymnal. For Church, School, and Home, ed. O. Hardwig. Chicago: Wartburg Publishing House, 1918.

---

[64] Compiled by the Unitarian and Universalist Commissions on Hymns and Services.

Henry Francis Lyte, Abide with Me; Fast Falls the Eventide

Worship His Majesty. Alexandria, Indiana: Gaither Music Company, 1987.

The Worshiping Church. A Hymnal. Carol Stream, Illinois: Hope Publishing Company, 1990.

HISTORY OF CHRISTIAN HYMNODY

1. Samuel J. Rogal, *Praise God from Whom All Blessings Flow*: A Sung Prayer of the Christian Tradition

2. Nancy James, *In Your Mercy, Lord, You Called Me* : A Sung Prayer in the Christian Tradition

3. Charles Parsons, *Pange Lingua*: A Sung Prayer of the Christian Tradition

4. Samuel J. Rogal, *Eternal Father, Strong to Save*: A Sung Prayer of the Christian Tradition

5. Robert B. Pierce, *A Stable-Lamp is Lighted*: A Sung Prayer of the Christian Tradition

6. Samuel J. Rogal, *All Hail the Power of Jesus' Name*: A Sung Prayer of the Christian Tradition

7. Samuel J. Rogal, *Recessional: A Victorian Ode (God of Our Fathers, Known of Old*: A Sung Prayer of the Christian Tradition

8. Samuel J. Rogal, *Rock of Ages, Cleft for Me*: A Sung Prayer of the Christian Tradition

9. Samuel J. Rogal, *Abide With Me; Fast Falls the Eventide*: A Sung Prayer of the Christian Tradition

10. Samuel J. Rogal, *O For a Thousand Tongues to Sing*: A Sung Prayer of the Christian Tradition

11. Samuel J. Rogal, *Onward Christian Soldiers*: A Sung Prayer of the Christian Tradition

Samuel J. Rogal

Dr. Samuel Rogal (Emeritus) was the Chair of the Division of Humanities and Fine Arts at Illinois Valley Community College, Oglesby, Illinois. The author of many books and articles, he has published several specialized monographs on John Wesley with The Edwin Mellen Press, including *John Wesley's London: A Guidebook* (1988); *John Wesley's Mission to Scotland, 1751-1790* (1989); *John Wesley in Ireland* (1993); and *John Wesley in Wales, 1739-1790* (1995). He also compiled a well-received reference set, the 10-volume *Biographical Dictionary of 18th-Century Methodism* (The Edwin Mellen Press, 1997-2000).

www.ingramcontent.com/pod-product-compliance
Lightning Source LLC
Chambersburg PA
CBHW021003230426
43666CB00005B/265